The Camping Kitchen: 50 Outdoor Recipes

By: Kelly Johnson

Table of Contents

- Campfire Chili
- Grilled Veggie Skewers
- Foil Packet Garlic Butter Salmon
- Dutch Oven Beef Stew
- One-Pot Pasta Primavera
- Campfire Quesadillas
- Cast Iron Skillet Cornbread
- Bacon-Wrapped Hot Dogs
- Campfire Nachos
- S'mores Dip
- Fire-Grilled Pizza
- Breakfast Burritos
- Foil Packet Chicken and Veggies
- Grilled Pineapple Rings
- Campfire Mac and Cheese
- Sausage and Potato Hash
- Dutch Oven Lasagna
- Campfire Banana Boats
- Chili Lime Shrimp Skewers
- Fire-Roasted Corn on the Cob
- Pancakes on the Griddle
- Grilled Portobello Mushrooms
- Campfire French Toast
- Kabobs with Teriyaki Sauce
- Campfire Hot Cocoa
- Lemon Herb Grilled Trout
- Campfire Apple Crisp
- Foil Packet Tacos
- Charcoal-Grilled Burgers
- Fire-Roasted Sweet Potatoes
- Campfire Popcorn
- Dutch Oven Chicken Pot Pie
- BBQ Pulled Pork Sandwiches
- Breakfast Skillet with Eggs and Bacon
- Grilled Zucchini Boats

- Smoky Campfire Beans
- Chocolate Chip Skillet Cookie
- Fire-Grilled Pork Chops
- Campfire Sliders
- Herb-Crusted Grilled Fish
- Campfire Veggie Stir-Fry
- Cinnamon Roll Skewers
- Spicy Grilled Sausages
- Sweet and Savory Campfire Kebabs
- Grilled Cheese Sandwiches
- Campfire Clam Bake
- Smoky Grilled Asparagus
- Trail Mix Energy Bars
- Campfire Tofu Scramble
- Dutch Oven Peach Cobbler

Campfire Chili

Ingredients:

- 1 lb (450 g) ground beef or turkey
- 1 medium onion, diced
- 1 red bell pepper, diced
- 2 cloves garlic, minced
- 1 can (15 oz/425 g) diced tomatoes
- 1 can (15 oz/425 g) kidney beans, drained and rinsed
- 1 can (15 oz/425 g) black beans, drained and rinsed
- 1 can (6 oz/170 g) tomato paste
- 1 cup (240 ml) beef or vegetable broth
- 1 tbsp olive oil
- 2 tsp chili powder
- 1 tsp ground cumin
- 1 tsp smoked paprika
- ½ tsp cayenne pepper (optional, for heat)
- Salt and black pepper to taste
- Optional toppings: shredded cheese, sour cream, green onions, tortilla chips

Instructions:

1. **Prepare Your Fire:** Set up a campfire or use a portable camping stove. Place a cast-iron skillet or pot over medium heat.
2. **Cook the Meat:** Heat the olive oil in the skillet or pot. Add the ground beef or turkey and cook until browned, breaking it up with a spoon. Drain excess fat if necessary.
3. **Sauté Vegetables:** Add the diced onion, red bell pepper, and garlic to the skillet. Cook for 3-5 minutes until softened and fragrant.
4. **Build the Base:** Stir in the tomato paste, chili powder, cumin, smoked paprika, cayenne pepper (if using), salt, and black pepper. Cook for 1-2 minutes to toast the spices.
5. **Add Liquids and Beans:** Pour in the diced tomatoes, kidney beans, black beans, and broth. Stir well to combine.
6. **Simmer:** Cover the pot and reduce the heat. Let the chili simmer for 20-30 minutes, stirring occasionally. If it becomes too thick, add a splash of water or broth.
7. **Serve:** Ladle the chili into bowls and top with your favorite garnishes. Serve with crusty bread or tortilla chips for dipping.

Grilled Veggie Skewers

Ingredients:

- 1 zucchini, sliced into rounds
- 1 yellow squash, sliced into rounds
- 1 red bell pepper, cut into chunks
- 1 yellow bell pepper, cut into chunks
- 1 red onion, cut into chunks
- 8-10 cherry tomatoes
- 2 tbsp olive oil
- 1 tsp garlic powder
- 1 tsp dried Italian herbs
- Salt and black pepper to taste

Instructions:

1. Preheat the grill to medium heat.
2. Thread the vegetables onto skewers, alternating colors and textures.
3. In a small bowl, mix olive oil, garlic powder, Italian herbs, salt, and pepper. Brush over the skewers.
4. Grill skewers for 10-12 minutes, turning occasionally, until vegetables are tender and lightly charred.
5. Serve warm as a side or main dish.

Foil Packet Garlic Butter Salmon

Ingredients:

- 4 salmon fillets
- 4 tbsp unsalted butter, melted
- 3 cloves garlic, minced
- 1 lemon, thinly sliced
- 1 tbsp fresh parsley, chopped (optional)
- Salt and black pepper to taste
- 4 large pieces of aluminum foil

Instructions:

1. Preheat the grill or oven to 375°F (190°C).
2. Lay out the foil sheets and place a salmon fillet in the center of each.
3. Mix melted butter and minced garlic, then pour over each fillet.
4. Season with salt and pepper, then top with lemon slices.
5. Fold the foil tightly around the salmon to create a sealed packet.
6. Cook on the grill or in the oven for 12-15 minutes, or until the salmon flakes easily with a fork.
7. Sprinkle with parsley and serve.

Dutch Oven Beef Stew

Ingredients:

- 2 lbs (900 g) beef chuck, cut into 1-inch cubes
- 2 tbsp olive oil
- 1 onion, diced
- 3 carrots, sliced
- 3 potatoes, peeled and cubed
- 2 celery stalks, sliced
- 3 cloves garlic, minced
- 4 cups (950 ml) beef broth
- 1 cup (240 ml) red wine (optional)
- 2 tbsp tomato paste
- 2 tsp Worcestershire sauce
- 1 tsp dried thyme
- 1 tsp dried rosemary
- 2 tbsp all-purpose flour
- Salt and black pepper to taste

Instructions:

1. Heat olive oil in a Dutch oven over medium heat. Brown the beef in batches, seasoning with salt and pepper. Remove and set aside.
2. In the same pot, sauté the onion, garlic, and celery until softened.
3. Add tomato paste and flour, stirring to coat the vegetables. Cook for 1-2 minutes.
4. Deglaze the pot with red wine (if using), scraping the browned bits. Add beef broth, Worcestershire sauce, thyme, and rosemary.
5. Return the beef to the pot, then add carrots and potatoes. Bring to a boil, then reduce to a simmer.
6. Cover and cook on low heat for 1.5-2 hours, stirring occasionally, until beef is tender and stew thickens.
7. Adjust seasoning as needed and serve hot with crusty bread.

One-Pot Pasta Primavera

Ingredients:

- 12 oz (340 g) pasta (spaghetti or penne)
- 3 cups (720 ml) vegetable broth
- 2 cups (480 ml) water
- 1 cup cherry tomatoes, halved
- 1 zucchini, sliced
- 1 yellow squash, sliced
- 1 cup broccoli florets
- 2 cloves garlic, minced
- 1 tsp olive oil
- 1 tsp Italian seasoning
- Salt and pepper to taste
- Parmesan cheese for topping

Instructions:

1. Combine pasta, broth, water, tomatoes, zucchini, squash, broccoli, and garlic in a large pot.
2. Drizzle olive oil and sprinkle with Italian seasoning, salt, and pepper.
3. Bring to a boil, then reduce heat and simmer for 10-12 minutes, stirring occasionally, until pasta is cooked and liquid is absorbed.
4. Serve with Parmesan cheese on top.

Campfire Quesadillas

Ingredients:

- 4 large flour tortillas
- 2 cups shredded cheese (cheddar or Mexican blend)
- 1 cup cooked chicken, diced (optional)
- ½ cup diced bell peppers
- ½ cup diced onions
- Olive oil for brushing

Instructions:

1. Lay a tortilla flat and sprinkle with cheese, chicken, peppers, and onions. Top with another tortilla.
2. Brush the outside of the tortillas with olive oil.
3. Cook on a hot griddle or cast iron skillet over the fire for 2-3 minutes per side, until golden and cheese is melted.
4. Slice and serve with salsa or guacamole.

Cast Iron Skillet Cornbread

Ingredients:

- 1 cup cornmeal
- 1 cup all-purpose flour
- 1/4 cup sugar
- 1 tbsp baking powder
- ½ tsp salt
- 1 cup buttermilk
- 2 eggs
- ¼ cup melted butter

Instructions:

1. Preheat a cast iron skillet over the fire.
2. Mix dry ingredients in one bowl and wet ingredients in another. Combine both.
3. Pour batter into the hot skillet and cook over indirect heat for 20-25 minutes, until golden brown.
4. Slice and serve warm with butter or honey.

Bacon-Wrapped Hot Dogs

Ingredients:

- 8 hot dogs
- 8 slices of bacon
- 8 hot dog buns
- Condiments of choice

Instructions:

1. Wrap each hot dog with a slice of bacon and secure with toothpicks.
2. Grill over the fire until bacon is crispy and hot dogs are cooked, about 8-10 minutes.
3. Serve in buns with your favorite toppings.

Campfire Nachos

Ingredients:

- Tortilla chips
- 2 cups shredded cheese
- 1 cup black beans, drained
- 1 cup cooked chicken or ground beef (optional)
- ½ cup diced tomatoes
- ¼ cup sliced jalapeños
- ¼ cup sour cream (optional)

Instructions:

1. In a cast iron skillet or foil tray, layer chips, cheese, beans, and toppings.
2. Cover with foil and cook over the fire for 10-15 minutes, until cheese melts.
3. Serve hot with sour cream or salsa.

S'mores Dip

Ingredients:

- 1 cup chocolate chips
- 1 cup mini marshmallows
- Graham crackers for dipping

Instructions:

1. Add chocolate chips to a cast iron skillet and top with marshmallows.
2. Cook over the fire until marshmallows are golden and chocolate is melted.
3. Serve with graham crackers for dipping.

Fire-Grilled Pizza

Ingredients:

- Pizza dough (store-bought or homemade)
- 1 cup pizza sauce
- 2 cups shredded mozzarella cheese
- Toppings of choice (pepperoni, veggies, etc.)

Instructions:

1. Roll out pizza dough and place it on a grill grate over the fire. Cook one side until firm.
2. Flip the dough, add sauce, cheese, and toppings.
3. Cook until cheese melts and crust is golden.

Breakfast Burritos

Ingredients:

- 4 large flour tortillas
- 6 eggs, scrambled
- 1 cup cooked sausage or bacon, crumbled
- ½ cup shredded cheese
- ½ cup diced bell peppers
- ½ cup diced onions

Instructions:

1. Lay tortillas flat and layer with scrambled eggs, sausage, cheese, peppers, and onions.
2. Wrap tightly and cook on a griddle or skillet over the fire for 2-3 minutes per side.
3. Serve warm.

Foil Packet Chicken and Veggies

Ingredients:

- 4 boneless chicken breasts
- 2 cups diced potatoes
- 1 cup diced carrots
- 1 cup broccoli florets
- 4 tbsp olive oil
- 1 tsp garlic powder
- Salt and pepper to taste

Instructions:

1. Place chicken and veggies on large foil sheets. Drizzle with olive oil and sprinkle with garlic powder, salt, and pepper.
2. Fold foil tightly to seal packets.
3. Cook over the fire or on a grill for 25-30 minutes, flipping halfway through, until chicken is cooked and veggies are tender.

Grilled Pineapple Rings

Ingredients:

- 1 fresh pineapple, peeled and sliced into rings
- 2 tbsp brown sugar
- 1 tsp cinnamon
- 1 tbsp melted butter

Instructions:

1. Preheat the grill to medium heat.
2. In a small bowl, mix brown sugar, cinnamon, and melted butter.
3. Brush pineapple rings with the mixture on both sides.
4. Grill for 2-3 minutes per side until golden and caramelized.
5. Serve as a snack or dessert.

Campfire Mac and Cheese

Ingredients:

- 12 oz (340 g) elbow macaroni, cooked
- 2 cups shredded cheddar cheese
- 1 cup milk
- 2 tbsp butter
- ½ tsp garlic powder
- Salt and pepper to taste

Instructions:

1. Place cooked macaroni in a cast iron skillet or foil pan.
2. Add butter, milk, garlic powder, and cheese. Mix well.
3. Cover with foil and heat over the fire for 10-15 minutes, stirring occasionally, until cheese is melted and creamy.
4. Serve warm.

Sausage and Potato Hash

Ingredients:

- 4 sausages, sliced
- 4 medium potatoes, diced
- 1 onion, diced
- 1 bell pepper, diced
- 2 tbsp olive oil
- 1 tsp smoked paprika
- Salt and pepper to taste

Instructions:

1. Heat olive oil in a cast iron skillet over the fire.
2. Add potatoes and cook for 8-10 minutes, stirring occasionally.
3. Add sausage, onion, and bell pepper. Cook until potatoes are golden and veggies are tender.
4. Season with paprika, salt, and pepper. Serve hot.

Dutch Oven Lasagna

Ingredients:

- 1 lb (450 g) ground beef
- 1 jar (24 oz) marinara sauce
- 9 lasagna noodles, broken into pieces
- 2 cups ricotta cheese
- 2 cups shredded mozzarella cheese
- 1 cup grated Parmesan cheese

Instructions:

1. Cook ground beef in a Dutch oven until browned. Drain excess fat.
2. Add marinara sauce and stir. Layer noodles, ricotta, mozzarella, and sauce mixture in the Dutch oven.
3. Repeat layers until ingredients are used, ending with mozzarella and Parmesan.
4. Cover and cook over coals for 45-60 minutes, rotating occasionally, until noodles are tender and cheese is bubbly.

Campfire Banana Boats

Ingredients:

- 4 bananas
- ½ cup chocolate chips
- ½ cup mini marshmallows
- ½ cup crushed graham crackers

Instructions:

1. Slice bananas lengthwise, leaving the peel intact.
2. Stuff the bananas with chocolate chips, marshmallows, and graham cracker crumbs.
3. Wrap each banana in foil and cook over the fire for 5-10 minutes.
4. Unwrap and enjoy with a spoon.

Chili Lime Shrimp Skewers

Ingredients:

- 1 lb (450 g) shrimp, peeled and deveined
- 2 tbsp olive oil
- 1 tsp chili powder
- Juice of 1 lime
- Salt and pepper to taste

Instructions:

1. In a bowl, mix olive oil, chili powder, lime juice, salt, and pepper. Toss shrimp in the marinade.
2. Thread shrimp onto skewers and grill over medium heat for 2-3 minutes per side, until pink and cooked through.
3. Serve with lime wedges.

Fire-Roasted Corn on the Cob

Ingredients:

- 4 ears of corn, husked
- 4 tbsp butter
- 1 tsp garlic powder
- Salt and pepper to taste

Instructions:

1. Rub corn with butter and season with garlic powder, salt, and pepper.
2. Wrap each ear in foil and roast over the fire for 10-15 minutes, turning occasionally.
3. Unwrap and serve hot.

Pancakes on the Griddle

Ingredients:

- 1 ½ cups pancake mix
- 1 cup water
- ½ tsp vanilla extract (optional)
- Butter for greasing

Instructions:

1. Heat a griddle over the fire and grease with butter.
2. Mix pancake batter according to package instructions.
3. Pour batter onto the griddle and cook until bubbles form on the surface, then flip and cook until golden.
4. Serve with syrup, fruit, or toppings of choice.

Grilled Portobello Mushrooms

Ingredients:

- 4 large portobello mushroom caps
- 2 tbsp olive oil
- 2 tbsp balsamic vinegar
- 1 tsp garlic powder
- Salt and pepper to taste

Instructions:

1. Remove stems from mushrooms and brush caps with olive oil and balsamic vinegar.
2. Season with garlic powder, salt, and pepper.
3. Grill over medium heat for 5-7 minutes per side, until tender and charred.
4. Serve as a side dish or burger substitute.

Campfire French Toast

Ingredients:

- 8 slices of bread
- 4 eggs
- 1 cup milk
- 1 tsp vanilla extract
- 1 tsp cinnamon
- Butter for greasing
- Maple syrup or powdered sugar (optional)

Instructions:

1. Whisk eggs, milk, vanilla, and cinnamon in a bowl.
2. Dip each bread slice in the mixture, coating both sides.
3. Grease a griddle or skillet with butter and place over the fire.
4. Cook the bread until golden brown on both sides.
5. Serve with syrup or powdered sugar.

Kabobs with Teriyaki Sauce

Ingredients:

- 1 lb (450 g) chicken, beef, or tofu, cubed
- 2 bell peppers, chopped
- 1 onion, chopped
- 1 zucchini, sliced
- ½ cup teriyaki sauce
- Skewers

Instructions:

1. Thread meat or tofu and veggies onto skewers.
2. Brush with teriyaki sauce.
3. Grill over medium heat for 10-15 minutes, turning and basting with more sauce, until cooked through.

Campfire Hot Cocoa

Ingredients:

- 4 cups milk
- 4 tbsp cocoa powder
- 4 tbsp sugar
- 1 tsp vanilla extract
- Whipped cream or marshmallows (optional)

Instructions:

1. Heat milk in a pot over the fire.
2. Stir in cocoa powder, sugar, and vanilla until well combined.
3. Pour into mugs and top with whipped cream or marshmallows.

Lemon Herb Grilled Trout

Ingredients:

- 2 whole trout, cleaned
- 1 lemon, sliced
- 2 tbsp olive oil
- 2 tsp fresh rosemary or thyme
- Salt and pepper to taste

Instructions:

1. Stuff trout with lemon slices and herbs.
2. Brush with olive oil and season with salt and pepper.
3. Grill over medium heat for 5-7 minutes per side until flaky.

Campfire Apple Crisp

Ingredients:

- 4 apples, sliced
- ½ cup brown sugar
- ½ cup oats
- 1 tsp cinnamon
- 2 tbsp butter, melted

Instructions:

1. Place apple slices in a foil packet.
2. Mix brown sugar, oats, cinnamon, and butter, then sprinkle over apples.
3. Seal the packet and cook over coals for 15-20 minutes until tender.

Foil Packet Tacos

Ingredients:

- 1 lb (450 g) ground beef or turkey
- 1 taco seasoning packet
- 1 cup shredded cheese
- 1 cup diced tomatoes
- 1 cup chopped lettuce
- Tortillas

Instructions:

1. Brown the meat with taco seasoning in a skillet or foil pan over the fire.
2. Serve meat in tortillas with cheese, tomatoes, and lettuce.

Charcoal-Grilled Burgers

Ingredients:

- 1 lb (450 g) ground beef
- 1 tsp garlic powder
- 1 tsp onion powder
- Salt and pepper to taste
- Burger buns and toppings (lettuce, tomato, cheese, etc.)

Instructions:

1. Mix beef with seasonings and form into patties.
2. Grill over charcoal for 4-5 minutes per side, depending on desired doneness.
3. Serve on buns with toppings of choice.

Fire-Roasted Sweet Potatoes

Ingredients:

- 4 sweet potatoes
- 2 tbsp butter
- 1 tsp cinnamon
- Salt and pepper to taste

Instructions:

1. Wrap each sweet potato in foil.
2. Place in the hot coals and cook for 40-50 minutes, turning occasionally.
3. Slice open, add butter, and season with cinnamon, salt, and pepper.

Campfire Popcorn

Ingredients:

- 1/4 cup popcorn kernels
- 2 tbsp vegetable oil
- Salt to taste
- Heavy-duty aluminum foil

Instructions:

1. Place popcorn kernels, oil, and a pinch of salt in a large sheet of foil. Fold into a pouch, leaving room for the popcorn to expand.
2. Secure the edges tightly and attach to a stick or place on a grill grate over the fire.
3. Shake gently over the fire until popping slows down. Remove and carefully open.

Dutch Oven Chicken Pot Pie

Ingredients:

- 2 cups cooked chicken, shredded
- 1 cup frozen mixed vegetables
- 1 can (10.5 oz) cream of chicken soup
- 1 can refrigerated biscuit dough
- Salt and pepper to taste

Instructions:

1. Preheat the Dutch oven over hot coals.
2. Mix chicken, vegetables, and soup in the Dutch oven. Season with salt and pepper.
3. Place biscuits on top of the mixture. Cover and cook for 20-30 minutes, rotating the oven occasionally, until biscuits are golden and cooked through.

BBQ Pulled Pork Sandwiches

Ingredients:

- 1 lb (450 g) pulled pork (pre-cooked or leftovers)
- 1 cup BBQ sauce
- 4 sandwich buns
- Optional toppings: coleslaw, pickles

Instructions:

1. Heat pulled pork in a skillet over the fire, stirring in BBQ sauce.
2. Toast sandwich buns over the fire if desired.
3. Assemble sandwiches with pork and toppings of choice.

Breakfast Skillet with Eggs and Bacon

Ingredients:

- 4 slices of bacon
- 4 eggs
- 2 medium potatoes, diced
- Salt and pepper to taste

Instructions:

1. Cook bacon in a cast iron skillet over the fire until crispy. Remove and set aside.
2. Add potatoes to the skillet and cook in the bacon grease until tender.
3. Crack eggs over the potatoes and cook until whites are set.
4. Crumble bacon on top and season with salt and pepper.

Grilled Zucchini Boats

Ingredients:

- 4 zucchini, halved lengthwise
- 1 cup marinara sauce
- 1 cup shredded mozzarella cheese
- 1/2 cup breadcrumbs
- Salt and pepper to taste

Instructions:

1. Scoop out the centers of the zucchini to create "boats."
2. Fill each boat with marinara sauce and top with cheese and breadcrumbs.
3. Wrap in foil and grill over medium heat for 10-15 minutes until tender.

Smoky Campfire Beans

Ingredients:

- 1 can (15 oz) baked beans
- 1/2 cup BBQ sauce
- 1/4 cup chopped bacon (optional)
- 1 tsp smoked paprika

Instructions:

1. Combine beans, BBQ sauce, bacon (if using), and smoked paprika in a small pot.
2. Heat over the fire, stirring occasionally, until hot and bubbling.

Chocolate Chip Skillet Cookie

Ingredients:

- 1 cup all-purpose flour
- 1/2 cup butter, melted
- 1/2 cup brown sugar
- 1/4 cup white sugar
- 1 egg
- 1 tsp vanilla extract
- 1/2 tsp baking soda
- 1 cup chocolate chips

Instructions:

1. Mix all ingredients in a bowl until combined.
2. Spread the dough evenly in a greased cast iron skillet.
3. Place over the fire, cover with foil, and cook for 15-20 minutes until golden brown.

Fire-Grilled Pork Chops

Ingredients:

- 4 pork chops
- 2 tbsp olive oil
- 1 tsp garlic powder
- 1 tsp smoked paprika
- Salt and pepper to taste

Instructions:

1. Rub pork chops with olive oil and season with garlic powder, paprika, salt, and pepper.
2. Grill over medium heat for 4-5 minutes per side, until fully cooked.

Campfire Sliders

Ingredients:

- 1 lb (450 g) ground beef
- 1 tsp onion powder
- Salt and pepper to taste
- Slider buns
- Optional toppings: cheese, pickles, ketchup, mustard

Instructions:

1. Mix ground beef with onion powder, salt, and pepper. Form into small patties.
2. Cook patties on a grill grate or in a skillet over the fire for 2-3 minutes per side.
3. Assemble sliders with buns and desired toppings.

Herb-Crusted Grilled Fish

Ingredients:

- 4 fish fillets (such as trout or bass)
- 2 tbsp olive oil
- 1 tsp dried thyme
- 1 tsp dried rosemary
- 1 tsp garlic powder
- Salt and pepper to taste
- Lemon wedges

Instructions:

1. Brush fish fillets with olive oil and season with thyme, rosemary, garlic powder, salt, and pepper.
2. Grill over medium heat for 3-4 minutes per side, or until fish flakes easily with a fork.
3. Serve with lemon wedges for squeezing.

Campfire Veggie Stir-Fry

Ingredients:

- 2 tbsp vegetable oil
- 1 red bell pepper, sliced
- 1 zucchini, sliced
- 1 onion, sliced
- 1 cup snap peas
- 2 tbsp soy sauce
- 1 tsp sesame oil
- Salt and pepper to taste

Instructions:

1. Heat oil in a skillet or Dutch oven over the fire.
2. Add vegetables and cook, stirring occasionally, until tender (about 8-10 minutes).
3. Stir in soy sauce, sesame oil, salt, and pepper, and cook for an additional 2-3 minutes.

Cinnamon Roll Skewers

Ingredients:

- 1 can refrigerated cinnamon rolls
- Skewers

Instructions:

1. Preheat the grill or fire pit.
2. Thread cinnamon rolls onto skewers.
3. Grill over medium heat, turning frequently, until golden brown and cooked through (about 8-10 minutes).
4. Drizzle with the included icing and enjoy.

Spicy Grilled Sausages

Ingredients:

- 4 spicy sausages (such as chorizo or jalapeño)
- 1 tbsp olive oil
- 1 tsp paprika
- 1 tsp garlic powder
- Salt and pepper to taste

Instructions:

1. Preheat the grill or fire.
2. Brush sausages with olive oil and season with paprika, garlic powder, salt, and pepper.
3. Grill sausages for 5-7 minutes per side until cooked through and slightly charred.

Sweet and Savory Campfire Kebabs

Ingredients:

- 1 lb (450 g) chicken, beef, or tofu, cubed
- 1 pineapple, cubed
- 1 red bell pepper, chopped
- 1 onion, chopped
- 1 tbsp honey
- 1 tbsp soy sauce
- 1 tbsp olive oil
- Salt and pepper to taste

Instructions:

1. Thread meat or tofu and vegetables onto skewers, alternating with pineapple.
2. Mix honey, soy sauce, olive oil, salt, and pepper in a bowl and brush the kebabs with the marinade.
3. Grill over medium heat for 10-15 minutes, turning occasionally, until cooked through.

Grilled Cheese Sandwiches

Ingredients:

- 8 slices bread
- 4 slices cheese (such as cheddar or Swiss)
- 4 tbsp butter

Instructions:

1. Butter one side of each bread slice.
2. Place cheese between two slices of bread, buttered side facing out.
3. Grill in a skillet or over the fire for 2-3 minutes per side until golden and the cheese is melted.

Campfire Clam Bake

Ingredients:

- 2 lbs (900 g) clams, scrubbed
- 1 lb (450 g) small potatoes, halved
- 4 ears of corn, husked and halved
- 1 lemon, quartered
- 4 tbsp butter
- 2 tbsp Old Bay seasoning

Instructions:

1. Place clams, potatoes, corn, and lemon wedges in a large piece of heavy-duty aluminum foil.
2. Add butter and sprinkle with Old Bay seasoning.
3. Seal the foil and cook over hot coals for 20-25 minutes until clams open and potatoes are tender.

Smoky Grilled Asparagus

Ingredients:

- 1 bunch asparagus, trimmed
- 2 tbsp olive oil
- 1 tsp smoked paprika
- Salt and pepper to taste

Instructions:

1. Toss asparagus with olive oil, smoked paprika, salt, and pepper.
2. Grill over medium heat for 5-7 minutes, turning occasionally, until tender and slightly charred.

Trail Mix Energy Bars

Ingredients:

- 2 cups rolled oats
- 1 cup mixed nuts (almonds, cashews, etc.)
- 1/2 cup dried fruit (raisins, cranberries, etc.)
- 1/4 cup honey
- 1/4 cup peanut butter
- 1 tsp vanilla extract

Instructions:

1. Mix oats, nuts, and dried fruit in a bowl.
2. Heat honey and peanut butter in a small pan over the fire until melted and smooth.
3. Stir in vanilla extract and pour over the oat mixture.
4. Press into a lined pan and refrigerate for 1 hour before slicing into bars.

Campfire Tofu Scramble

Ingredients:

- 1 block firm tofu, crumbled
- 1 tbsp olive oil
- 1/2 onion, chopped
- 1 bell pepper, chopped
- 1 tsp turmeric
- Salt and pepper to taste

Instructions:

1. Heat olive oil in a skillet over the fire.
2. Add onion and bell pepper, cooking until softened (about 5 minutes).
3. Stir in crumbled tofu, turmeric, salt, and pepper.
4. Cook for an additional 5-7 minutes, stirring occasionally, until heated through.

Dutch Oven Peach Cobbler

Ingredients:

- 1 can (15 oz) sliced peaches, drained
- 1 box yellow cake mix
- 1/2 cup butter, melted
- 1/2 cup water

Instructions:

1. Place peaches in the bottom of a greased Dutch oven.
2. Sprinkle cake mix evenly over the peaches, then pour melted butter over the top.
3. Pour water over the mixture and cover with the Dutch oven lid.
4. Cook over coals for 30-40 minutes, until the top is golden and a toothpick comes out clean.

www.ingramcontent.com/pod-product-compliance
Lightning Source LLC
LaVergne TN
LVHW081508060526
838201LV00056BA/3005